OVERCOMING PROCRASTINATION

LIFE CHANGING HABITS TO CURE PROCRASTINATION FOREVER

TABLE OF CONTENTS

Bonus: Free Procrastination Busting Tool

When you subscribe to my newsletter via email, you will get a FREE article on an important procrastination-busting tool called time boxing. All you have to do is click on the link and enter your email address to get it right away. As well, I'll send you sneak peeks of my upcoming books.

Get Access Now!

or

Click here it's FREE.

Or your can access it here:
http://www.nathanandsarahtaylor.com/free-tips-from-nathan/

INTRODUCTION

I want to thank you and congratulate you for downloading the book, "Overcoming Procrastination: Life Changing Habits to Cure Procrastination Forever".

This book contains proven steps and strategies on how to overcome procrastination and become more productive.

Almost all of us procrastinate one way or another. However, not all of us make procrastination a way of life. If you are one of these people, you know how difficult overcoming procrastination is - it is like stopping a moving train from its tracks. Overcoming procrastination goes beyond the issue of time management. And this book will show you make positive changes in your life that will help you achieve your goals.

Thanks again for downloading this book, I hope you enjoy it!

Respective authors own all copyrights not held by the publisher.

The information herein is offered for informational purposes solely, and is universal as so. The presentation of the information is without contract or any type of guarantee assurance.

The trademarks that are used are without any consent, and the publication of the trademark is without permission or backing by the trademark owner. All trademarks and brands within this book are for clarifying purposes only and are the owned by the owners themselves, not affiliated with this document.

CHAPTER 1

THE ENEMY CALLED LATER

"I'll do it later."

Have you ever heard yourself say this - maybe not only once, but countless times already? And along with this sentence comes a hundred creative reasons why you'd rather do something later than now. Maybe you're really very busy or you are still trying to figure out how to start? Or maybe you'd rather watch your favorite TV show first than start working on your project immediately? You can think of a hundred more different reasons why you keep putting off doing an important project but the end result is the same - you end up regretting why you have decided to do something later except of now.

The condition called 'LATER' or what we very commonly know as PROCRASTINATION. However, procrastination is more than just simply saying later. As the Merriam-Webster Online Dictionary defines it, procrastination is the habit of putting off something that should be done INTENTIONALLY and HABITUALLY.

Procrastination affects different types of people no matter what the age, gender, race, profession, family background, or status they have. In fact, 20 percent of the population admits they are chronic procrastinators. In college alone, a whopping 95 percent of students procrastinate on their academic responsibilities. Furthermore, procrastination is also one of the top reasons why those who are taking their Ph.Ds. fail to complete their dissertations. Procrastination seems harmless but if you look at the different studies and research regarding procrastination, its causes, and its effects, it is also one of the major causes of stress and some health problems. It is also one of the reasons of failed relationships and missed opportunities. If such bad effects come from it, why do people still do it? Is it just out of sheer laziness or is there something else?

Diagnosing the Cause

Procrastinators are often wrongfully accused as being lazy and disorganized. Worst, a lot of people think that procrastinators simply don't care enough to do something immediately. On the contrary, procrastinators are often hardworking and smart people who are fully capable of doing the job but can't seem to do it on time.

So, if it is not laziness, what is the cause of procrastination, then? And why do people procrastinate when they know full well the regret and anxiety of not doing what should have been done? It's a classic case of 'me knowing what is wrong and I need to stop but I just seem can't.'

You know what to do but it seems you're waiting until the last minute to do it. What happens then is that you keep on repeating the vicious cycle of 'LATER' and you feel distressed and anxious. If you are someone who often procrastinates, try answering the questions below and answer 'YES' if the situation mirrors you or your behavior and 'NO' if it doesn't.

Do you often find yourself thinking that the task you're doing can suddenly all go wrong?

Are you always worried how people, especially your family and friends, will react at your failure?

Are you afraid of trying something new because you might fail?

Are you afraid of success because of the additional responsibilities that come with it?

Do you always think that if you do well, people will have much higher expectations from you?

Do you believe success will reveal the real you?

Do you believe in doing everything perfectly?

Do you have difficulty in persisting when things aren't going right?

Is it better not to do something than doing it imperfectly?

A YES answer to the first three questions reveals that your procrastination stems from your fear of failure. You procrastinate and avoid doing a task because you think that you will still fail despite all the effort you put into a task.

On the other hand, if you gave a YES answer to the next three questions reveals your fear of success rather than of failure. You procrastinate even though you know you can do it and even succeed in doing it because you are protecting yourself from the bigger responsibilities and higher expectations that come with success.

Lastly, a YES answer to the last three questions reveal perfectionism as the underlying cause of your procrastination. Because you want to get things done perfectly, you set up high standards that are impossible. In turn, you feel frustrated and end up not doing anything.

Have you ever heard yourself saying this? Maybe not just once, but countless times already? Well, the good news is you are not alone because studies have shown that

A Much Deeper Reason

Aside from the reasons stated above, procrastination can also be an indication of deeper, inner conflicts where it involves a specific person or event. For example, a person will procrastinate when he is assigned a task because the person who gives him the task reminds him of a significant "other" in his past who seems to threaten his ego.

Procrastination can also be a sign of a personality disorder characterized by fear and anxiety. Those who are suffering from such disorders use procrastination so they have full and perfect control of their situation and environment. Some examples of these disorders are passive personality disorder where a person uses procrastination, intentional forgetfulness and inefficiency, and stubbornness to express his or her aggression covertly.

In a study made between the relationship of psychological disorder and procrastination, those who often procrastinate are placed in a higher risk for depression and other maladaptive behaviors. It can also be a result of a neurological deficiency or damage. However, despite these relationships, procrastination in itself is a maladaptive behavior that needs to be addressed.

CHAPTER 2

UNBOXING PROCRASTINATION

"If you know the enemy and know yourself, you need not fear the result of a hundred battles." This is what the great military strategist, Sun Tzu, said in his book The Art of War. The same applies if you want to overcome the habit of procrastination.

Just like any enemy, procrastination comes in many faces so it can be quite sneaky. Moreover, procrastination can be good for you, especially if the adrenalin rush of doing something at the last minute spurs you into action and stimulates your creativity. By being able to identify which is good and which is bad for you, it is easier to create an action plan to defeat the enemy.

Am I a Procrastinator?

Each one of us has procrastinated at certain points to avoid something unpleasant or difficult. It is all about willpower where you set manageable goals and the euphoric feeling of being able to beat deadlines. However, if you do not start now, there's a very big possibility that it can get worse tomorrow. As Dr. William Knaus, co-author of the book Overcoming Procrastination: Do It Now -- How to Break the Procrastination Habit puts it, "procrastination is an automatic process which results in needless postponements and keeps repeating itself again and again.

If you want to know if you are a procrastinator, look at the following symptoms of procrastination.

You focus on low-priority tasks first before doing the most important ones because you either find them boring or you feel you are incapable of finishing the task.

- You switch between tasks without finishing them.

- You tend to do tasks that are not even on your to-do list.

- You often delay your decision reasoning out that you need to research more or the idea needs time to ripen.

- You are constantly checking your email and social media accounts.

- You want to do something immediately but you are trying to find an easier way to do it.

- You often tell yourself or others that you can perform much better under pressure; thus, delaying things until the last minute.

- You often say that you are uninspired at the moment, you are tired, or you need something to motivate you.

- You put yourself in a situation that you cannot finish. For example, you convince yourself that you have a fatal flaw causing you to foreclose on yourself before you can even start.

- Or you often use the past as an excuse saying you don't understand it and you need to examine your life more closely.

- You always feel the need to weigh your options leaving you undecided until you end up not starting anything.

The Dangerous Effects of Procrastination

There are certain character traits that seem to encourage procrastination. Some of the common traits shared by procrastinators are impulsiveness, being easily distracted, adherence to irregular sleep schedules, and erratic social rhythms.

More often than not, a lot of people, especially procrastinators themselves, already know the regret they will feel afterwards when they continually put things off. However, it seems that they have difficulty getting out of the vicious cycle or they have not realized the dangerous effects of procrastination.

What starts as a harmless distraction becomes full-blown. It begins with a simple, "I'll catch up with my e-mails or I'll check my Facebook notifications for a minute." But what becomes a minute becomes an hour or even a number of hours.

If regret is not enough reason to stop procrastination, then its effect in every aspect of your life should be a wake-up call to get out of the rut. In fact, if procrastination becomes chronic, it can even ruin your life. One example is people who wait before going to the doctor until something serious has developed or disabled them. If they had come earlier, the problem could have been resolved much faster.

In a 2003 study titled, "I'll Look After My Health, Later" which was published in the Personality and Individual Differences journal, Timothy Pychyl and his fellow researchers have established that procrastination can not only affect a person's health, but also his well-being and quality of life. What spurred Pychyl and his collaborators to focus on procrastination was the 1997 study conducted by two Florida State University Psychologists, Roy Baumeister and Dianne Tice. The two psychologists divided two groups of university students - those who procrastinate and a control group of average university students. Both group of students were healthy at the beginning of the term but at the end of the term, those who procrastinated became less healthy than those who were in the control group. Furthermore, the procrastinators also became more stressed than their average counterparts.

Here are some of the consequences of procrastination that might affect the different aspects of your life.

Physical:

- Health problems can worsen when left unattended

- Sleep problems, such as insomnia

- Fatigue

- Restlessness

- Tension and high blood pressure

- Headaches

Emotional:

- Irritability

- Frustration

- Depression

- Anxiety

- Guilt

Mental and Cognitive:

- Low self-esteem

- Perfectionism

- Self-criticism

- Obsessive Compulsiveness

- Mental Fatigue

Career:

- Productivity

- Missing career opportunities and promotions

- Inability to contribute effectively to the team or company

- Likelihood of accidents and mistakes in the workplace

- Career burnout

Relationships:

- Relationship becomes full of tension

- Constant nagging and frustration

- Isolation and helplessness

Aside from the enumerated consequences above, procrastinators might also feel a sense of lack and emptiness as if life happened and passed them by. This could develop into a pessimistic attitude towards the future and worse, can lead to depression.

Chapter 3

When Lists are not Effective

You might think that one of the most effective ways to handle procrastination is to create a to-do list because it gives you reassurance that you are somehow organized and that you have a sense of priority. However, to-do lists could be your downfall - something that could worsen your procrastinating habits. Here are some of the reasons why to-do lists won't work to cure procrastination.

Bluma and Her Theory

Bluma Ziegarnik was a Russian psychologist who observed in 1927 that waiters could remember unpaid orders much better than the paid ones. After they have completed the task, they were unable to remember the details of their order. This led to her theory that we store things in our short-term memory and we have to keep on remembering them lest they die out like candlelight snuffed by the wind.

The same effect happens, as people tend to remember uncompleted tasks rather than the completed ones after a long period of time. Therefore, you keep on thinking about the uncompleted task until you receive closure.

Similarly, if you create a to-do list in the hopes of regaining control will leave you with the same feeling of guilt, dread, and anxiety when you are unable to finish the tasks on the list within the time-scale. In reality, you only created a short-term solution instead of a long-term one.

The Tyranny of Choice

In his book, The Tyranny of Choice, Barry Schwartz echoes the same observation as Ziegarnik saying that a number of choices can leave more problems and create more negative emotions. In a complementary research made by Sheena Iyengar, the study revealed that our brains become overwhelmed when the options exceed to more than seven. She said that you could decide more easily and quickly when given fewer options. Thus, looking at the 20 or more tasks on your to-do list will further spur you to procrastinate where reading your email becomes more desirable than doing actual work.

Diverse Complexity and Priority

A to-do list will always consist of different tasks with varying time frame and levels of difficulty. Thus, you will often find yourself 'prioritizing' a 33-minute task to a 3-hour project to give you a false sense of satisfaction thinking that you have crossed out something from your list. This is still focusing on a low priority task to a high priority one.

Furthermore, your list also comprises tasks with varying priorities where you will tend to focus more on your A priorities than your B priorities, until B becomes an A priority. But when does B or C become an A priority? Does that mean that if your car maintenance is in your B priority, you will putt off doing it until it becomes an A priority - when your car breaks down in the middle of nowhere in an unlikely hour? This is still procrastination putting you in a very dangerous situation.

The Lack of Context

When you enumerate various tasks on a piece of paper, each one of them looks the same - a three or four-line phrase. They don't capture the importance of each task nor do they display the vital information you need, such as the amount of time you need for each task. But the most important question of all is: How much available time do you have? If your answer to this question is unclear, then you will have trouble making an intelligent decision on what you should be working on first.

The Story of General Han Xin

General Han Xin was one of the great military strategists in Chinese history and was given the title as one of the "Three Heroes of the Early Han Dynasty." He served under Liu Bang and became instrumental in expanding the Han emperor's realm by using innovative strategies.

One of these strategies was assembling his troops with a river behind them allowing no room for retreat. The ploy worked because they gained victory as the soldiers fought fiercely to survive since they had no other choice left.

The same thing applies to how you beat procrastination. Simply creating a to-do list will not guarantee that you will stop procrastinating. In fact, to-do lists are geared more likely towards failure and frustration because they don't really let you do the most important tasks. The reason for this is because these lists do not have a commitment device, a tool that locks you to perform a course of action even though it is unpleasant but one that produces a desired result.

A commitment device leaves you no room to do other things but the most important task at hand. Just what General Han Xin did to his troops where the only choice is to fight back or face death in the hands of their enemy or death by drowning in the river behind them.

For example, if you are saving up for retirement but you often find yourself spending what you should be saving, you should set up automatic deposits so your savings are taken directly from your monthly paycheck. Thus, even if you don't feel like depositing money to your savings, you don't have a choice because it is automatic.

CHAPTER 4

DIFFERENT STROKES FOR DIFFERENT FOLKS

No two individual are the same and the same goes with procrastinators. Thus, you cannot suggest the same solution to two different people. Dr. Joseph Ferrari, one of the leading researchers on procrastination and the author of the book Still Procrastinating: The No Regrets Guide to Getting it Done, has identified the different types of procrastinators into three categories - the thrill seeker, the avoider, and the indecisive procrastinator.

Do you feel that you work best under pressure? Are you confident that you can produce high quality work? Do you feel relaxed about deadlines? If you answer yes to all three, then you are the Thrill Seeker-type of procrastinator.

If you are someone who is afraid of failure or success, then you are the Avoider-type of procrastinator. The Indecisive-type, on the other hand, is a perfectionist who is afraid of making decisions.

To understand each of these categories much better and where you fall among them, you need to take a closer look at their behavior and characteristics. And along with each characteristic are suggestions how to tackle the issue.

The Thrill Seeking Procrastinator

Aside from their usual "I work best under pressure" alibi, the thrill seeking-type of procrastinator often delay doing their tasks because they are looking for the adrenaline rush of racing against the clock. They are what psychologists label as sensation seekers.

Individuals who have arousal-based personality traits often fall in this category because they want to feel stimulated at the optimal level of their arousal. Therefore, they delay tasks in order to get the rush they want at the last minute to be at their optimal level of arousal. That is why, as existing research reveals, thrill seekers actively look for stimulating activities even if they are negative situations just to feel more thrill or stimulation.

On the other hand, the "working better under pressure" alibi can also mask another face of the thrill seeking procrastinator. In a situation where a person may feel guilty because he believes that he should be working on a task but isn't, there might be a tendency to rationalize the cognitive dissonance he feels because his actions don't match his beliefs. Thus, there is a need to resolve the mental tension between working and not working by adopting the "I work better under pressure" attitude in an attempt to make sense of their delay.

If you are this kind of procrastinator, you can still get the rush you want from doing positive tasks. Instead of focusing on getting stimulated by the deadline rush, why not get the rush of finishing the project early? Do you find the task difficult and unpleasant? Find creative ways to make the task look more interesting so you can finish it before deadline. After that, celebrate your victory of being able to finish early by throwing a party for your friends. This should make you excited and stimulated.

To make the task more exciting, create rewards that provide

instant gratification, such as checking your Facebook. Although it is a fact that such activity is also a cause of procrastination, it is much better to include it as a reward than curbing the urge to do so which makes the urge much stronger until it explodes. Divide tasks into smaller tasks and shorter deadlines and set up rewards.

The Avoider Procrastinator

This type of procrastinator is afraid of both failure and success. They are always concerned about what others might think and shy away from an unpleasant or high stake task. Avoiders are afraid to expose their incapability, real or imagined, that they put off doing a task by masking it with a lack of effort. This makes them feel better because they avoid blame by doing so.

Instead of avoiding the task, challenge those irrational thoughts that stop you from making a decision to act by keeping a daily journal. Most of the time, the things that you tell yourself to putt off doing are not relevant to the task. Instead, they are connected to the emotions or feelings you have about performing the task or about the outcome if you finish the task. Keep a journal and write down your thoughts. Then, challenge them by asking questions, such as what could be the worst thing that will happen if you finish a certain task? It's adaptive and constructive for you to identify what your strengths and weaknesses are. If you keep on avoiding self-discovery and decision-making, you won't be able to live your life to the fullest.

Another area where avoider procrastinators suffer from is decision fatigue simply because of a lack of exercise using their decision making muscle.

The key to overcoming this is by making simple decisions and then gradually progress to more complex decisions to build your multi-thinking strength. Just as an athlete builds his muscle strength to train for a marathon, the only way to strengthen your decision making muscle is to make decisions frequently. Do not let fear of potential failure paralyze you to become an avoider. Instead, continue to consciously focus on making decisions by yourself and focus on the successes of your endeavors.

The Indecisive Procrastinator

One of the common traits of indecisive procrastinators is perfectionism. While perfectionism can spur you to do something excellently, it affects the indecisive in a negative way. Because of fear of failure and being criticized for a mistake, an indecisive ends up not doing anything. As Dr. Ferrari states in his book, indecisive procrastinators do not finish their task because they are afraid of people evaluating their abilities. What these types of procrastinators want is people judging their efforts and not their capabilities.

What makes indecisive procrastinators unique is that they are not just afraid of failure and criticisms, but they are also afraid of success. That is because they are afraid that when they succeed, people will expect more from them. Either way, it's a lose-lose situation for these types.

So how do you overcome perfectionism? It is not enough to know that your perfectionism is hurting you, but you need to recognize as well that your perfectionism will not earn you extra sympathy from people every time you procrastinate.

In addition, you also need to focus on the bigger picture instead of the finer details. By being aware of the bigger objective, it is easier to prioritize on what you should do.

CHAPTER 5

THE HOW AND WHEN OF BEATING PROCRASTINATION

Nike puts it effectively in their slogan, **Just Do It.**

In order to beat procrastination, you need to act on it. However, it is not enough that you know it, but you also need to know how and when to do it. The overall goal is to take one step at a time but there are different ways to approach each step. Some steps may be effective in some tasks, while others may not be relevant. Try them and see which method works best for you.

Worst First - The idiom grab the bull by its horns is the goal of this step. This means that you do the most difficult and most dreaded tasks first and the other tasks that follow will be much easier.

Take Advantage of Momentum - You can also start doing a task you really like and finish doing it without taking a break. Gaining momentum and continuing to go forward without breaking it is a good motivation.

The 5-minute Tasks - If you feel overwhelmed about doing a certain task, try spending 5 minutes on each task. Then reassess after five minutes if you are still up to it for another five minutes. If five minutes feels shorter after doing the exercise for quite some time, you can make the chunks larger, like 10 or 15 minutes. You will be surprised how easy it would become to finish the task once you get the ball rolling.

Create Time Limits - Another effective approach to beat procrastination is to set a time limit to a certain task. This might prove effective if you are a thrill seeking procrastinator because you will be pressured to finish the task before the set deadline you gave the task. This method will be more effective if you set the time limit to a shorter time, you may be more willing to go further.

Choose the Right Time and the Right Place - You must learn to respect how your body works. This means that if you feel more creative and productive at night, then schedule to do your task in the evening as long as it is not time dependent. Aside from time, it is also important to choose the right place to perform a certain task. Be aware which environment makes you more productive and which surrounding gives you a lot of distractions.

Remind and Keep in Sight - If one cause of your procrastination is forgetfulness, set up reminders where you can see them to remind yourself of the task at hand. Don't let the tasks be out of your sight so that it won't be out of your mind. Create post-it notes, diaries, email managers, and other things that will remind you of the task.

Plan Rewards - To make your tasks become more pleasant and exciting, create rewards after you finish each task. Just make sure that the rewards you give yourself are guilt-free. This means that you have to pre-plan the rewards and fit them around the work that needs to be done. The more you set up rewards for each of your achievements, the more likely you will feel less deprived of something; thus, the less likely you will procrastinate. Just make sure you balance achievements and pleasure so that you will become a doer than a procrastinator.

Finding the Right Time

Overcoming procrastination isn't just about knowing the methods, but also finding the right time when to do it. This involves creating a routine and place the tasks you keep on putting off fall into the slots of your routine. That means you have to allocate your time to work on your goals that can be done in two ways - scheduling and unscheduling your task.

Scheduling is like keeping a detailed journal of your daily or weekly tasks. It includes creating a plan of what needs to be done and at what point in your day or week. Also include a plan when you should do the steps for each task and the goals you have been procrastinating on.

The downside of scheduling, however, is that spontaneous events can get in the way of the planned events. If you are one of those who find it difficult get back on track once unscheduled events interfere with your plans or you might feel that your week is too regimented and planned, then you can try to unschedule.

Unscheduling works the same way as scheduling but instead of writing down your tasks, you write down the time when you are free. Thus, you can place the tasks you usually procrastinate on during the free time you have during the day or week. Doing things this way, you can't fail at the unschedule, since you have not set any specific target. In addition, interruptions are more easily accommodated, and you feel like there is some spontaneity in your week. At the end of each day or week, you can look back and see how much time you have devoted to doing things you have been procrastinating about, by looking at the blocks of time you have marked off.

CHAPTER 6

WHERE SELF-CONTROL COMES IN

Behind procrastination is the problem of self-control or will power. All people have self-control but why is it others have stronger willpower than others? What's the secret? Roy Baumeister, a Florida State University psychologist who was also responsible for the 1997 study about procrastination, conducted an experiment that allows subjects to exercise their self-control. His experiment reveals that self-control is a quality that can be exhausted.

This means that self-control is similar to a muscle that you can exercise and improve. When you exercise self-control for the first time, it might be difficult. But if you make a conscious effort to exercise your willpower on a daily basis on different situations, you will soon discover that it becomes much more easier as time goes by.

Strengthening Self-Control

If self-control is a muscle, how can you strengthen it? And if it can be exhausted, how can you conserve it?

One of the most common and effective methods of strengthening your self-control is to avoid temptation. This was proven in the marshmallow study conducted by Walter Mischel where kids who stared directly at the marshmallow were less likely to resist it than those who closed their eyes or distracted their attentions away from the marshmallow.

This out of sight, out of mind principle proves to be effective in adults as well. In one recent experiment, office workers who have candies on their desks tend to eat more candies than those who keep theirs in their drawers.

Another effective strategy to strengthen self-control is through implementation intention. This method involves intention that take the form of if-then sentences to help you plan for situations that are likely to weaken your resolve. For example, an employee who is trying to curb his procrastination might say before he puts off the task, "If the job feels difficult, then I will break it into shorter minutes." Research has shown that this method is effective even among those whose self-control has been exhausted by lab tasks. It goes to show that having a plan of action ahead of time lets you make a decision without exerting too much of your self-control.

Taking One Step at a Time

The same way you strengthen your self-control muscles through daily exercise, the same activity can also fatigue it. In order to avoid hurting it, you need to start making changes in something small.

In a study conducted at the Macquarie University in Sydney, scientists discovered that smokers who practiced self-control by avoiding sweets for two weeks showed more progress than those who didn't. Aside from being able to curb smoking, they also showed improvement in almost all areas of their lives.

For example, you can begin by doing the 5-minute task stated earlier in the book. From there, you also set manageable goals and think through a plan how to achieve them. It is not only less stressful, but it can also be fun.

CONCLUSION

Procrastination has some serious effects in every aspect of your life if you leave it unaddressed. Learn to be aware of your behavior patterns so you can properly identify and address those that are causing you to procrastinate. Don't just focus on one method, but try each one until you find a method that is effective yet you are comfortable with. You can still feed your procrastination urge by making your tasks more interesting and creative.

Thank you again for downloading this book!

I hope this book was able to help you to overcome procrastination.

Finally, if you enjoyed this book, then I'd like to ask you for a favor, would you be kind enough to leave a review for this book on Amazon? It'd be greatly appreciated!

Click here to leave a review for this book on Amazon!

http://tinyurl.com/pra5joo

Thank you and good luck!

Nathan Taylor

Preview Of 'DIY Organizing and Cleaning: The Easiest, Quickest Hacks to Declutter Your Home and Life' by my wife Sarah

Clutter is stagnant energy. Whenever there is clutter in your house, there is also clutter in you whether it is physically, emotionally, or mentally. In fact, clutter tells more about who you are as a person. Here are a few of the most common.

- If your house is filled with the stuff of other people, it means that you do not know how to say no to others. You allow people to invade your own personal space and have trouble setting boundaries.

- If a lot of old stuff lies around your room or house, you have a tendency to be nostalgic about it and blame the past for your present situation.

- A house filled with rarely used or never-been-used things reflects fear of the future because you tend to stuff yourself just in case you might need them. It also signifies that you aspire to do or be something you're not.

- Unfinished projects, such as half-finished remodels and half-completed art suggest perfectionism and fear of failure.

How Clutter Affects Your Brain

Whether your office desk is filled with piles of paper or your closet filled with old clothes, excessive stuff all around you can have a negative effect on you ability to focus and process information. This was according to a research conducted at Princeton University involving people in organized and disorganized environment. Neuroscientists said that the physical clutter all around you takes away your focus and attention from the task at hand resulting in low productivity and performance as well as high levels of stress.

In another research done by a team from UCLA found out that a mother's stress hormones increase as they deal with their possessions. The study, which involved 32 families in Los Angeles, concluded that physical clutter overloads your senses stressing you out and decreasing your performance and creativity. It is similar to how multitasking affects your brain.

How Clutter Affects Your Life

Professional organizers who have been hired to organize cluttered homes and offices often hear the same complaints from their clients - drained energy, failure to locate things lost in the mess, and clutter beginning to get in the way of their lives. A similar survey also revealed that those who have cluttered homes and offices dread going home or working because the clutter simply gives them a feeling of suffocation.

Aside from being non-functional and non-productive, here are other things how clutter affects your life.

- **Money** - If you don't organize your bills, receipts, and other financial documents, you can lose them in the pile. The result? Late or missed payments not to mention the stress of sorting through the piles of paper. In addition, buying more similar items just because can also put a strain on your budget.

- **Time** - How does clutter affect your time? You spend a great amount of it just trying to find lost items amid the clutter.

- **Health** - As your clutter accumulates, so does dust and other stuff, like animal dander, and mold which can lead you to develop allergies. If you have asthma or allergies, you are increasing your risk .

- **Safety** - People in cluttered homes say that they have difficulty navigating through staircases or floors littered with clutter. There is the possibility you might trip over. Aside from that, you are also making your living or working space a fire hazard candidate.

- **Clutter and Stress** - The home is primarily a haven of rest but clutter can make it a source of your stress. The stress comes from anxiety how others perceive you as they visit your house. Because of this, it can also cause you to have lower self-image.

Click here to check out the rest of DIY Organizing and Cleaning: The Easiest, Quickest Hacks to Declutter Your Home and Life on Amazon.

Or go to: http://amzn.to/1rOw62O

BONUS: FREE PROCRASTINATION BUSTING TOOL

When you subscribe to my newsletter via email, you will get a FREE article on an important procrastination-busting tool called time boxing. All you have to do is click on the link and enter your email address to get it right away. As well, I'll send you sneak peeks of my upcoming books.

Get Access Now!

or

Click here it's FREE.

Or your can access it here: http://www.nathanandsarahtaylor.com/free-tips-from-nathan/